What Haunts Me
the Most

ALSO BY CHIMEN GEORGETTE KOURI

Peach Milk

Advance Praise

"The rhythm in these macabre and seductive poems is like a sorceress dancing under a full moon and Chimen Georgette Kouri is casting a spell in *What Haunts Me the Most*. The images of cicadas, frogs, and swans; the tower and the hanged man; blood and guts; the fragile egg cracked open by ruinous fingers; the familial hauntings of a dead grandmother and the constant daily deaths of girlhood, devouring men, and being the eldest daughter grab hold of you like the branches of pine trees clutch at the dress of the final girl as she runs. Why does she run? To learn how to let go, to learn how to be? These poems ask how to survive when it's our blood on the knife. They had me by the jugular."

—Alise Versella, author of *Tender is the Body* and *When Wolves Become Birds*

"In this eerie yet alluring collection, fate stalks our hesitant heroine through the dark forest of a gothic fairytale, dread looming as she crawls towards the threshold from wounded girlhood to ambivalent womanhood, the Maiden willing herself into the Crone. Weaving beauty into viscera, enchantment into decay, Kouri challenges the doubtful notion of maternal instinct in a world with teeth and a taste for flesh, where eldest daughters are tasked with purifying the psychic waste of generational trauma at the cost of their own innocence. In *What Haunts Me the Most*, creamy flowers bloom from rancid meat, blood drips and congeals as dreams devour, true crime warps the pastoral scenery, nostalgia betrays survival; you cannot dare to look away, breathless and left wanting more."

—Frankie Balzano, author of *Spider Rodeo*

"Chimen Georgette Kouri's *What Haunts Me the Most* is a courageous dissection of girlhood and what it means to be haunted by it. Her pieces aren't afraid to place the female body under a microscope in order to view the atoms that make up both purity and wickedness and witness them dancing and intertwining. There's an all-encompassing curiosity and an intuitive wisdom present in each of her poems, which leaves the reader questioning what it means to be a daughter in a home that sometimes feels like a prison."

—Jessica Ballen, author of *Kosher*

What Haunts Me the Most

Chimen Georgette Kouri

QUERENCIA PRESS

© Copyright 2023
Chimen Georgette Kouri

ISBN 978 1 959118 80 0

www.querenciapress.com

First Published in 2023

Querencia Press, LLC
Chicago IL

Printed & Bound in the United States of America

To my grandmother, Loretta
I hope one day we can laugh about all of this

Contents

I just know when he stuffed his hands in his pockets, said
Okay. Couldn't hurt to try? and shuffled back to his roadside stand
to arrange his jelly jars and stacks of buckets, I had made
a terrible mistake. I just know my summer would've been
full of pies, tartlets, turnovers—so much jubilee.

—Aimee Nezhukumatathil – *The Woman Who Turned Down a
Date with a Cherry Farmer*

Part One

the ongoing whispers of every meat hook reminding me why I'm here:
to hunt the fat hog.

Tell Me About Yourself

The interviewer asks me to describe myself. I'm sitting across from him, knees pushed together, back straight. I look down at my hands; I know I can gut him like a fish if I don't get this job. I open my mouth, my tongue covered in bitter-tasting vomit.

I want to assure him that I brushed my teeth after throwing up, but instead, I describe myself as...

Danger

Danger [dan-ger] n.

The possibility of suffering harm or injury.

Deer in my peripheral vision. Swallowed infants inhabiting the stomach of Cronus. My grandmother receiving chemotherapy but continuing to prepare for the worst. Crows devouring the memory of my father releasing the pet rabbit into the marshland. My mother watching from afar, her disapproval ghostly. Neighborhood boys playing Russian Roulette. His body slacking against the tree. The apparition kissing him in the woods. The maternal instinct. The Tower. The child's arm remaining a swan's wing. Dissected animals cradled in the hands of students who believe they're invincible. *Why do I hear screaming in the night?*

Rejection

Neighborhood boys explore the marshland behind my house. They exude rapacity, looking to find treasure buried next to careless graves of pets or inside the trunks of barren trees falling into the wetland. Instead, they uncover a bloated rat hiding underneath a baseball cap, hissing and running away.

The slow-moving clouds refuse to release the sun from captivity. I climb the fence and look over my shoulder, afraid my parents will punish me for my curiosity, the maggots in their dreams revealing themselves.

I assume I will crush the remains of a rabbit with my feet; instead, I fall into a pile of leaves. Something grasps my ankles and pulls me under like a great-white gripping a swimmer's leg.

Should I carry a coin behind my lips as I'm taken across the river? Holy water dripping from above, my tongue eager for a taste.

As my body plunges deeper into the mound of death, the boys ignore me, their attention focused on a two-headed frog they wish to split in half.

A List Describing Home

I

Honeysuckles grow in the spring, their sweet fragrance wafting in the wind. I pluck the flower and slurp its nectar until my stomach aches, its sugary taste disregarding a mouthful of candy, the cavities needless and contemptible.

II

A woman with red hair haunts me in my sleep and lurks in my bedroom doorway in the early morning. Is she lost, searching for Treasure Lake? Locals believe pirates buried treasure in the lake centuries ago, but they could only find a pair of ice skates left behind during winter when the lake turned to ice. Maybe the lake is meant to bring her to her final purpose: Hell.

III

The beach remains desolate. Severed fish heads bake beneath the merciless sun. A dead seagull lays on its back, wings spread, waiting for the ocean's waves to drag it to its darkest depths. Hospitals dump used syringes and garbage into the water, eventually soiling the sand. The weather grows harsh. Violent hurricanes remove most of the shore, the restless ocean soaking the asphalt during heavy rainfall. I imagine the town will wash away one day, becoming an abandoned seaweed-infested habitation.

IV

A bird's nest resides on a tree branch in my front yard. I embrace the eggs in my hands every morning, eager to hear the babies cry. Their speckled turquoise eggshells remind me of gemstones I would keep in my pocket on the first day of school, hoping they would attract friends. I hold one of the eggs between my fingers, its fragileness like a helpless snowflake I catch on my tongue. Its shell cracks open, the slimy yolk oozing between my ruinous fingers. I don't know what to do but run.

White Ribbon

I

February 2003. My grandmother dies from lung cancer. I don't know how many people say goodbye to her, but I'm not one of them. Instead, I'm forced to attend my first sleepover, unaware I will never see my grandmother again.

Later that night, I sensed my friend and I weren't the only two in the room.

II

Thirteen years later, I'm sitting next to a man who predicts a future of wedding veils hanging from bedroom doors and rounded bellies resembling grassy mountaintops in the spring. He watches me and smiles, showcasing his dimples, a cigarette between his fingers. The smell reminds me of childhood mornings: my grandmother looking out the kitchen windows, smoking, the dawning sun shining through, her face remaining stoic. Whatever she was thinking of was never worth sharing.

III

I turn my attention back to the man and place my hand on top of his, the cigarette burning a hole into my palm. Will I say goodbye to him? Or will I be in another's bed, unable to sleep because Death stands over me, provoking me to acknowledge there is one less person on Earth I love?

Surrender

I

I didn't pray for my grandmother's safety the night of her funeral. She screamed my father's name, the piercing cry echoing throughout the house. Frightened, I turned to the woman babysitting me. She looked spooked but quickly dismissed me, her evident denial reminding me of a summer afternoon when I was swimming in a lake, my foot caught beneath a rock, a vicious flow willing to rid me of my body. They lifted me by my shoulders, threatened abandonment if I didn't relax, some prehistoric monster pulling me by my toes. Their voice held no panic, but their eyes revealed distress. I think of that memory often, wishing I had released myself from their restraint and allowed the lake to consume me.

II

Lying in bed between my parents that night, I couldn't silence the rumination regarding my grandmother's frightful scream, the darkness continuing its slaughter, my father the only one who could save her. But I didn't wake my father to tell him. I simply fell asleep.

What Haunts Me the Most

I always hear footsteps after the dawn's first hunt, a stranger exploiting the flames of an overworked incinerator. The warmth nudges me in the direction of a child's birthday party. Someone admits a humorous truth about worms crawling through eye sockets. An eternal promise was made: a cremation chamber, Her body taking three hours to disintegrate inside a cardboard box. Nothing can alter this fate; it's covered in spiderwebs, your candy necklace softened and wrapped around its wrist like rosary beads dangling beneath the sleeves of a praying nun. I stab a pig's heart with pins and needles and roast it over a fire, a charm to ward off fearsome witches. I wish I could permit a witch to hypnotize me with their hex, my sullen heart dismissing protective doves, a drawn-out ignorance like a woman who believes if she craves sweets, her swollen belly will produce a girl. A girl I will bury in the backyard beneath a rose-pink flower bed.

Who cares if I'm put to sleep like a dog? It won't matter if a honeybee forages inside the confessional booth, urging me to admit it wasn't an accident. The churchyard will always remain in the distance, the ongoing whispers of every meat hook reminding me why I'm here: to hunt the fat hog.

Playing Along

They mistake the animal trappings for nests, a coyote's foot caught and restrained. Your garbage Lolita falls to her knees, makes daisy chains, ties them into knots; blood in her mouth, no longer needed to swallow. The harvest moon reveals itself and reminds me why she was naked from the waist down, her body lying on a rock wall in a field a hundred yards away from her abandoned shoe, her red coat shielding her perpetrator's remorse: her jaw was too small to devour what it believed it could manipulate. *If I'm alone, why do I feel a warm breath on the back of my neck?* Her ghost remains noiseless, waiting for me to turn around and recognize her pale face, her timid expression when the ducks swam in the discolored water, a hemorrhage I couldn't clean fast enough. Sisters mutilate their feet to fit inside glass slippers; doves pluck their eyes out. I press my ear against her chest during the funeral; I hear a violent howl and pretend it belongs to the coyote.

Maiden in the Tower

What am I meant to be if not the stitch between us loosening or the candle always burning out before we can wish for a longer night? I'm limping toward my grief, but it turns into a rabid dog, snarling and exposing its fangs. I don't see a point in running; the dog will eat the moon, find me in my sleep. They can tear the house down, throw out the betrayal I abandoned in the backyard, and I will still think about you on your birthday. I will still think about your laughter when the dog chased me onto the bridge, and the only option I had was to jump, but I couldn't until I stopped caring about how cold the water was. Watch me; I can play victim too. I can demand you to turn around, even if I'm miles away. I can dream about my dead grandmother and believe I will solve the problem. Unlike you, when imprisoned in the Tower, I always find a way out. I always let down my long hair and pull up whatever was sent to save me.

Three Hail Marys

I can't be like her, an adolescent who watched Christ throw his head back and take her nipple and areola into his mouth. Instead, I am the mother who warns you to keep the shotgun away from the kitten.

I'm ridiculed for possessing the power to bleed, the thick lining of my uterus withdrawing from my womb, the warm home you abandoned after you discovered the attic door slightly open, never closed again.

You took a peek and liked what you saw: your father thrusting his fingers into a vanilla sponge cake, hurting me, eager to puncture your mouth like a hook attached to a fish slipping out of a river.

When your father dies, I won't turn my face to the wall or hold the back of my neck like my mother did when I threw up after touching a bird's feather I found in the woods. His death will force out a greater threat, like a stranger exposing themselves in the shadows.

My Path Is Littered With Mirrors Absent of My Reflection

Mirror 1

I tear my parents' wedding photos into tiny pieces like a child ripping the spread wings of a cicada, a summer sound diminished, comparable to when I pretend I've never fastened the dog's leash around His neck before, a hunger enabling me to feel closer to Heaven.

I shove the film down my throat, suffocating on the bridal bouquet, my mother's fragility held in the pockets of her bridal suit. Their courthouse betrothal preceded the umbilical cord wrapping around their newborn's neck like a rat snake coiling itself around its unhatched eggs, a baby beetle eating the snake embryos after they trap and relocate the mother.

Mirror 2

A frog stalks me in a meadow, beseeches me to press my lips against its sticky tongue, its bulging eyes resembling mushroom conks growing on dead forest wood, a contamination like childhood memories: Baby Soft perfume, your mother's dream journal revealing nightmares as unanswered prayers.

The frog defecates gold coins, a soiled trail guiding me to an oven preparing to broil my feasible dreams. *You want to become a writer?* Wash your clothes in the river and wait for the water to sheathe the bodies of lying virgins thrown from the cliff, their wasted flower crowns caught in the limbs of fallen branches on the river's edge like hair stuck in a shower drain, a lesson never learned.

Mirror 3

Finally, I see Him, a wound springing from my mother's silence before they killed the rabbit, an impulse similar to walking behind a pretty girl, wondering if she'll turn around in time or wind up in the river, a dog's chain wrapped around her throat.

He lights a candle for my grandmother inside a deteriorated church, its stone walls collapsed, ruined by a February blizzard. He prays my grandmother won't steer me in the direction of greed, my hands tied with the ribbons intended to bind our hands together to represent our amalgamation, a love so gentle it makes me recall the night after my brother was born; when my father and I laid in bed, and he wrapped his arms around me.

He knows what I taste like: a pair of underwear hastily washed in the sink; a package of latex condoms I'm allergic to; bedroom eyes no longer withheld in the bedroom; a white rose soaked in blood; a red strawberry spoiling fast.

Part Two

I would rather bob for apples,
bite into a red delicious carved with his name.

The Farmer's Wife

I choose the dream that will last as long as it takes to forgive my silence. Until the blackberries grow bitter. Until it is Christmas Eve, and He is crying at my grave. In this dream, I live where Jesus hasn't stopped suckling. Where I'm stalked in the woods and find refuge by pulling on my crone mask and offering whoever was following me an apple from my husband's farm. I've always wanted to be a farmer's wife, a woman who cooks breakfast with eggs her husband collected in a wire basket. Prepares a meat her husband once played with in the field. But watching this huntsman fall between the trees, choking on the Maiden's Blush apple, is enough to beget gratitude, like a child standing next to their father's hanging deer. They don't know why they're relieved to stand next to a dead thing; they likely believe they don't deserve the hunger.

Secrets

We're driving down a dirt road, the trees in the forest displaying uncanny shapes illuminated by the full moon's glow. Like a coward, you steal your father's car in the middle of his nightmare; when the soldiers dispose of the bodies of four virgins in a river, their spirits haunting fishermen and regretful mothers who refuse to provide milk for their infants. A Polaroid is taped to the dashboard: a bride, hunched over, her face shielded by her hands, compelling me to question whether she is crying or laughing. The road grows darker. The smell of wet grass lingers in the summer air. In the distance, I perceive blinding headlights buried deep in the forest, a stranger's shadow running between the spaces of the tall trees. Wherever you are taking me, I hope I will lie next to you with candy hearts dissolving on my tongue.

Sweetheart Theater

I'm sitting next to you in a sweetheart theater, watching a film about a man and a woman falling in love in a field of white roses, a milkmaid wrapped with bondage rope forgotten between the trees. Purity hides in their secondhand clothes, a Polaroid of their honeymoon torn and yellowed: a glimpse of angel wings in an outdoor fire.

My mother's whispers slither through the cracks in the walls, taunting me to admit how much I miss you. She uncovers the notes in my diary and reveals why I'm scared of waking up in the morning when my skin grows thinner every day.

The man and woman in the film dissect a sheep's uterus and cradle its ripening fetus. The taste in my mouth sours as I recall your childhood memories when you watched a stranger stalking your father's barn, looking to steal. Are your adolescent encounters the reason you experience nightmares where you embrace my body with a pull?

It doesn't matter. I will continue recommencing myself as I fly across the sky, proclaiming the end of nightmares, my rosy fingers opening Heaven's gates, dawn forcing its arrival.

When you grow old, I will turn you into a cicada, your deafening song lingering in the trees as I remain seated in this sweetheart theater, still fearful of what others might believe.

Faithful Daughter

I

I pull the knife on him after I lay seven different flowers underneath my pillow and don't dream about him. Instead, I dream I am a nun living in the 1400s, biting the other sisters of the convent. I don't know why or how the biting started, but I've learned it's best not to look out my window when my mother calls my name from the woods. When it's the dead of night, and she's sleeping beside me.

II

I don't recall killing the two-headed calf. I hold its skull and wish it would have been stillborn. Then, I wouldn't have had to hide the knife in the field, where the cornstalks are so tall you lose your way, even in the daytime. Isn't that the scariest? How nature can hurt you by implementing what it was created to do. How I doubt my grandmother's warnings in my dreams.

III

I'm told I have a strong name associated with a saint
who refused to turn her back on God. She watched as her
sons were beheaded, each of their bodies falling
forward, lifeless. I don't want to be self-denying. Don't I
deserve to wear a garland on my head, surrendered to
the truth that was patient enough to wait for me?
Wouldn't it be a violation to make me a widow before he
has taken a bite out of my rosiest peach? I watch an
opossum climb across a tree branch and know to wait
until the danger turns into a door. For how long, I'm not
sure. I guess until my anxiety grows too heavy, it starts
lactating, nursing me. In the meantime, I could go back
for the knife, remind myself it would have been worse if
I had tied a red sash around his arm. There would have
been no guarantee he would have returned, but at least I
would have known he would be waiting for me.

Selfish

I offer you roses picked from the garden, their yellow petals gaping and creamy.

The sun-drenched backyard provides me with the shrill dissonance of pretty-face maidens, their prairie dresses flowing in the wind, powder-blue fabric reminding me of coiled waves returning to the pitiless sea.

I pull brittle weeds from the dirt, wasting my dandelion wishes on warm weather and one hundred petals of a rose tasting insidious.

The bedsheets smell like a rotisserie chicken gone bad after I'm too uncomfortable to make eye contact, my legs on your shoulders, you pulling me deeper like children fighting over a toy.

You prefer to incinerate my girlhood:

- A decorative umbrella made of lace shielding the heated sun from burning me.
- Satin gloves trimmed with silk bows.
- A ruffled dress, piggy pink, comparable to JonBenét.

Our daughter places a classic all-white arrangement above my mother's grave, a cutie pie invoking little prayers.

She doesn't kiss the flowers like I do, a doll hospital eventually removing the rot I was born with, replacing it with flaccid legs and round cheeks, eager to be dropped on my face.

I lay in an open field, the grass cold and jaundiced, resembling an ache I can't hold onto, like a cotton swab damp with the residue of an unripe peach.

Where were you the day I found the roses plucked, revealing the loss of a game of she loves me, she loves me not?

Scopophobia

My childhood dreams swallowed the intention of allowing only one man to loosen the ribbons in my hair, an abundance of yellow tresses tangled amongst the bristles of a comb, like unraveled yarn trapped in the penetrating claws of a housecat.

Did I lie to my mother for nothing?

Of course not. There is always a reason why a girl must lie to her mother. Always an excuse regarding the heavy snow covered in blood, the slush engraved by tire tracks, their impressions like fingerprints, a mystery waiting to be solved.

If I find you crying on the kitchen floor, my knees will soften like a deer falling in the woods before its body is hanged upside down, its arteries draining. Between my legs, a strawberry blush.

I'll have no choice but to collect your tears in a teacup brimming with lilac seeds, a first love losing its petals, disoriented, like learning the sign of the cross for the first time, hesitant as to why an inverted cross holds the same meaning.

The sound of your persistent sucking elicits me to want to break your neck, a chicken prowling the farm without its head.

I am a rotten girl, forcing you to guard our expired crop, a dry harvest dismissing any growth of restoration.

Flannan Isles Lighthouse

The crushing force of an ocean escapes my sunburned lips. It creates puddles of shipwrecks poisoned with the secrets of Pirate Blackbeard, his decapitated head nestled between a siren's breasts, her groin resembling an oyster rejected for its buttery taste.

I dive into the bottomless puddles. Sea witches dance with the drowned carcass of my sweetheart, carnivorous seaweed slithering through their flowing, matted hair. I offer them my purity ring, but the trinket is worthless. I don't tell them why.

Infants sprout from seashells, suckling on Poseidon's trident, their toothless gums bleeding, the smell of rust conjuring a rape inside a virgin's temple, a needless punishment for a girl who foaled as she was dying.

Seafoam wraps around my throat. I drown in my diffidence like a fish cradled in a net, my body upended, exposing my pasty stomach.

My remembrance forces its way out of my throat. It falls to the ocean floor as I recall meeting my sweetheart in a lighthouse illuminated by a thousand candles, their scarlet flames revealing the desolation of loved ones who prefer the absence of my ghost.

Baby Steps

I promise the end of October will trust the serpentine stone lodged in my throat. There will be no fear when crossing the bridge. No feminine urge to hold a butcher knife when the beauty says, *"Imagine the water at night. Now imagine that water revealing the faces of your anger. Don't they all look dead?"* I still don't understand what it means to move on, to exit someone's life and refuse to smell the chum. Maybe if I meet the lighthouse keeper, he will guide me in the opposite direction of the storm to ensure I don't keep going back. Back when the horse looked like it had horns as it stood in the fog.

Tell Me About Yourself

Floral wallpaper peeling off the walls of my mother's bedroom. The humidity moistens me, and I have no choice but to remove myself from her walls, unable to look after her because I am merely a daughter, a girl with no say in the matter. *I've felt like this since I was born.* Red-haired ghosts cry as they watch the wallpaper peel, their trauma dumped into a lake to drown. *Wait till you see them violate my dreams and tear me to shreds.* I am a lonesome cherub, shooting an arrow into the heart of a man who cries when he leaves me. I sleep with an apple under my arm, persuading him to eat it the next day, and he guzzles it, choking on the core. *It's my fault for the way things are.* I ask God to cut me some slack, and he makes me upchuck in other people's sinks. I am a target. Prey. A sacrifice. I am fallen peaches rotting in the dirt, the sweltering hours of summer afternoons tiring a dog. I yearn to be bitten, my juices dripping down the chins of sweet boys. They use a chef's knife and cut me lengthwise, the blade hitting my pit. *It's the easiest way.*

I am innocence pleading for restoration in the afterlife. I sit next to you in a field of fresh daisies. *No.* I sit across from you in a poorly lit diner, our booth torn and sewed with doves' heads, our fingers tracing their lifeless beaks. *I'm crying, but this is the happiest moment of my life.* Lily of the Valley sprouts from my tears, its bell-shaped tepals used as drinking cups for fairies. *Wait! It's poison!* I am the Virgin crushing the serpent with my feet, my palms heavenward, signifying trust in a house of deception and grief. *The sound of heavy boots creaking against wooden staircases terrifies me.* Eager hands wrap around my throat. Bodies intertwine. My friends ask if it hurts, and I smile and ask if they believe in God. *Only when I bend my knees.* I am a Polaroid of your deceased grandmother hidden beneath your pillow like a prayer card; you think it will protect you. The last time she visited you in a dream, you drove her to the snow-covered woods and left her there. *Feed your lies to the wolves, the ones who bite like mothers.*

Six Pomegranate Seeds

What I hope for stalks me like vultures in the desert, awaiting my collapse: a blue-eyed man crouching in the creek, collecting gravel. I still provide it with milk, my breasts like a cow's udders hanging between its hind legs, its newborn calf suckling the swollen-pink gland resembling an undeveloped flower. I pray, but everything remains the same: I'm still wearing a rope leash around my neck, marching to the gallows. My mother says expectations are homemade, a natural impulse, a forgotten dream every girl but me left behind in their flaxen-hair youth. I burn the Hanged Man, his surrender nonexistent. I'm tired of having to sacrifice; they keep tricking me into eating pomegranate seeds. My longing rummages through the straw-like grass, a morning dew submitting itself to flimsy cobwebs bound to the overgrown weeds. Rats gnaw on the blooming daffodils, a birthday cake mistakenly placed beneath the perfidious sun. What I hope for softens in my hands like a child dying, like balloons caught in the leafless trees during winter.

How Deep Are Your Scars?

My mother was dragged out of the roller rink into the winter night, wearing nothing but a sequin dress, and what I like to imagine were Cinderella's glass slippers. In truth, they were scuffed high heels I watched her limp around in when she came home late at night, a stranger with her, heard but not seen, whispering in the dark, reminding me of cold wind when it isn't snowing.

When she looked at me, her face seemed distorted, scrunched up, and deepening with humiliation. I imagined her thin arms covered in bruises the following day.

My mother disappeared, the disco ball no longer forming sparkles in her eyes like antifreeze inside a snow globe, the mixture of liquids preventing snowflakes from descending too quickly after being shaken. I suppose somebody beat her in the backseat of a car or raped her on a motel bed.

She was in trouble for being pretty. For looking at men a certain way, my father said when I received a nightmare at dusk: my mother turning into a witch, chopping my brothers and me into tiny pieces for a spell intended to make her rich.

Now darkness inhabits beneath my eyes, a pack of smokes hanging in my father's shirt pocket. It's hard to look at my brother sometimes because he bears our mother's brown eyes.

I stand on the same roller rink floor.

Speed Bumps (The Royal Rat)

A woman rides past me on a bike, a baby in her arms. I watch as she crosses bridges made of cardboard, reminding me of a warrior who won't surrender until their tribe is safe.

As she approaches a house without doors, I observe the color of her bonnet, debating whether she is isolated or wed.

She disappears through a curtained portal. A crane hides in a shrub, a rodent's tail dangling from its beak.

For Tara Calico

I

Your mother agonizes over the Polaroid of you bound and gagged in the backseat of a van, your defiant eyes lacking hysteria.

No one believes the girl in the photo is you but your mother.

II

I have nightmares where I find your body perishing in the switchgrass, your hands curled like a newborn and tucked beneath your chin, afraid to enter a world where you are no longer attached to your mother, her milk unsweetened.

I lay next to your body and think of the slaughtered calf I found being picked by vultures on the side of a dirt road.

Like you, the calf wandered off from its mother, ignoring her warnings about men and their will to destroy when hungry.

Bow to Fate

I walked down the hill, carrying what I thought
were wildflowers the deer had dropped on my lap
when I could hold nothing but a father's skull.

Instead, I was gripping a tree's broken branch
in a storm, a flock of sheep moving farther than me.

If this is Death's way of betraying my future, I would rather
bob for apples, bite into a red delicious carved with his name.

Part Three

returning to the woods only to discover
the wolf doesn't want to devour you.

Premonition for the Devouring Female

My father searches the hollow cavities of a rotisserie chicken, his eager hands fissuring the carcass, tearing any remaining white meat, sucking on the bones. It reminds me of nature's endless cycle: tears becoming gnarled thorns, my secrets biting me behind my knees, returning to the woods only to discover the wolf doesn't want to devour you. I'm still tender, a cherry picker's affection remaining stiff between my legs; warm raindrops pelting an open-mouthed rose. I'm voiceless; always two fingers inserted in my mouth, pulling. Apple cores dangle like wind chimes, a reluctant destiny continuing to throw rocks into the wind. Can't you hear it? My rage is screaming in the woods like a red fox during mating season, a shrill noise comparable to a familiar whimper: human and female. *Don't worry*, it howls, a futile echo lost in a mass of sodden pine needles. *You're strong like your father.* I don't want to be strong; I want to be the same as a fawn curling itself next to its mother's broken neck, a gunshot in the distance causing it to shake.

The Horse in the Storm

I

The horse looks out into the storm, pays no attention to the sickle I hold behind my back. We're alone, the bridge made of splitting wood likely to collapse, our fate like Mary Magdalene wiping Jesus's feet with her hair: self-sacrifice. I don't want to imagine my empty womb: daughters unwillingly clinging to their mother's submission, sons wrestling for their father's reflection. I dream about rose quartz but don't feel ready to move on from these hollows that will eventually expand into a long line, a generational timeline concerning a female dog in heat, unaware of her release dripping onto the kitchen floor as she walks to her water bowl, panting and swollen.

II

When I had no choice but to violate benevolence, I found myself in the stable, naked in the hay, the horse raising its head and whickering at me as if to say, *Why do you keep holding yourself back?* If I allow myself to leave, what will consume me if not the expectations?

What will hold out its hand and abandon my clothes in the sunflower field? I was too scared to kill the horse then; I'm too attached now. Their counterfeit love is the only secret I nurture; no one ever believes the daughter.

III

The horse moves away from me, remains weary. The storm pursues, doesn't consider something bad is already happening here. I want the horse to look at me, to acknowledge why no one believes I should reject loyalty. But the horse's stare remains vacant like the emptiness I uncover when I lift my skirt and spread my thighs. *Here's your out. Leave if you want to.* I wish the horse would plunge headfirst inside me, galloping across my fresh daisies, wandering without restraint. If we reunite, I will approach it empty-handed, my ribbons attempting to hold up my desiccated breasts, a distant dream absorbing inside a parent's stomach and eventually excreted. Someday, I will be found swaddled with rope, floating in the river, a viable procedure ensuing prayers for the slain. I'm not afraid when the dog trembles at the foot of my bed, a violent storm rousing the trees in the woods to admit their iniquities before they fall.

The Final Girl

I

I'm refusing the closure at this point. I keep telling myself it's time to move on; the boys will always laugh at you, no matter how hard you try to change the story. I remain at the slaughterhouse, over-apologizing again. I don't mean to make him wait; between my legs becomes slick, my overlooked hole a disposal for heavy corpses like a sky burial providing food for vultures. The thick and boiled crimson no longer stains my underwear; only bugs feasting on raw eggs. I'm not sure what I'm gaining from this nightmare; I just know it's going to take a while for me to wake up.

II

Help. I think being the eldest daughter is becoming my personality trait. I don't know how to disregard guilt when my brother or sister fails; when my father finds his garden ruined, expecting to find a nest of baby rabbits behind the wire fence. Instead, he finds me naked in the dirt, my feet crushing his soft lavender.

He reminds me to question my existence; why my creative accomplishments are inadequate in his eyes, a man who had to leave because of war. Being the eldest daughter is similar to the Final Girl in a slasher movie; everyone has to die for you to survive. But I don't feel like the Final Girl. Not when it's my blood on the knife.

When Resentment Creates Delusions

Lately,

I've been grinding my teeth, my anxiety imbued with anger. My subconscious arrives at night, revealing nightmares of my teeth falling out of my mouth and landing in a wolf carcass buried beneath the snow.

Lately,

a clown hides in my closet, beckoning me to follow him deeper into the funhouse. I'm greeted by distorted mirrors, my face melting and dripping into puddles between my feet. I'm faceless, doubting the destination that follows forgiveness. The clown drinks my liquefied flesh, chews my eyeball, slurps the optical nerves like spaghetti. He tips his head back, reveals rotted teeth.

Lately,

I wake up every night to a man standing over me, staring into my face, his nose inches from mine. My face twists, revealing hysteria, a nightmare refusing to relinquish its apelike incubus. The man hurries to my window and waves his hands, motioning for me to keep quiet. I remain still until he disappears.

Someone is in my room! I yell into the darkness of the house. My father runs in, searches beneath my bed, confirms locked windows. The dog remains unfazed. He continues to sleep, his fangs hidden beneath black lips.

Full Harvest Moon

Do you think there is anywhere for me to run? I'm asking you because I can't rely on the sound of the windchimes when the breeze flows from the east. Each new day presents me with a mask I cannot swallow, one I cannot burn or drain the sand from. What does everyone expect from me when all I dream of is softness? The answers to all my begging? I think I was saved when the cat cuddled against my sister's arm; impotence will never surpass her. She can be bitter only for the right reasons: when her reflection validates a statement always spoken with regret. Whatever happens, I can still grow in the summer, start over in the fall. I know I don't belong here anymore; every time I think of leaving, a fortune cookie reads: *Did Dymphna forgive her father?* And I imagine her father's sword, how he thrust it as punishment, swung it to demonstrate what a daughter deserves when her mother is better off dead. I won't pretend I'm not angry, but I will hide the white flag on the fence post, the attraction, the past. I remember I can't swim; that's why I've been drowning in the deep end of this loyalty for so long. For now, I can watch the dogs run in the yard and bark at a turtle hiding in its shell. I can touch what needs to be touched. I can expect.

Possession

I

You cradle my body in the miry swamp, lavish vegetation surrounding us, common reeds and thick cattails titillating our skin. My wedding dress fades yellow in the blackest closet. The church bells chime; now we must deliver the Lord's Prayer: your tongue pursuing the sticky honeypot deep inside my throat.

Entries in my diary read, *"They're going to tell you to remove your teeth"* and *"Are you still scared?"* But no one is scared enough to question what I mean.

Polaroids of my grandmother scatter the hardwood floor, her well-rounded hips exposed. She stands beside a screen door, likely waiting for my grandfather to notice the swell in her stomach.

My mother says I inherited my grandmother's fingernails, how easily breakable they are.

After she died, my grandmother's body didn't wither; her skin failed to shrink. Her fingernails didn't grow, an illusion other dead hands fail to hide.

I open her urn, her ashes soft between my fingers, reminding me of snow blanketing my windshield when

I drove through the woods during a blizzard. I thrust my hands further inside the urn, eager to discover something else we share.

II

When you touch me, I remember thorns attached to wilted roses, anxious to draw blood. I hear the pastor dunking women into the filthy water, their white dresses exposing the shapes of their breasts, round and wideset like a predator's eyes observing a lamb keeping close to its mother.

The women sing cheerily like Manson girls showcasing a lack of remorse. They gnaw on indigestible jawbreakers, a swelling in their cheeks.

Prom invitations float above the water, crinkling beneath the torrid sun, a spring dance embodying a Clapton song. A king and queen, their formal attire, hangs from the tangled branches of a dead tree. An abundance of fresh corsages remains buried in the throats of girls who swallowed peach pits, their failed attempt to dispel hidden demons.

Did you know? We're not safe anymore.

III

I'm dressed like a bride on the hour of my exorcism, an autumnal evening intimating an unsettling wind. My veil hides me from evil spirits who wish to spoil my happiness. They use the door like everyone else, take off their shoes in the mudroom, remind themselves to take the backroads home.

I consider burying myself alive beneath the patio, faceup like my sister exiting our mother's womb, her head wedged against our mother's pubic bone. *I'm sorry I didn't feel safe after that.*

Before the ceremony, my mother brings me two large eggs in a rose-tinted candy dish. I pretend I can't break them, an ignorance I consider when I deep-throat the barrel of a shotgun.

The eggs crack, revealing baby swans. They sit in my palms, nibble at my skin, search for the warmth of their mother's wings. They don't attack me when I spread my legs in the grass, the soles of my feet black from walking barefoot in the woods.

Why did Zeus, in the form of these devoted creatures, take advantage of their purified state? He violated a woman, came at her with his jagged beak.

IV

I reminisce about my childhood days exploring a grassy meadow. The dirt chafed my knees, dimpled and sore. Jagged rocks nicked my skin. A locket hanging from my throat housed a chrysalis longing to release its winged butterfly.

I remember closing my eyes and picking daisies, daydreaming of a scarce bouquet. The number of daisies you pick is the age you will marry, a flower girl tossing petals, her innocence once belonging to the bride, but now the bride dresses unwillingly in red.

Maybe I would marry a man who wouldn't push me away when I needed to vomit. He would hold my hair, feed me saltine crackers, make sure I ate slowly.

Before I knew it, I plucked too many daisies. Sixty-one? Eighty-two? One hundred and nine? I would never be a young bride who tasted of baby-blue garters but an old hag who opened her legs and revealed cobwebs housing flies grappling with death.

V

People crowd the room as my body rises from the bed. My parents stand in the doorway, their mundane clothing altering into wedding attire they wore twenty-five years ago, a ruffled train soiled after my mother ran to the field and gave birth to the shattered version of my father.

Their nostalgia mocks me, penetrates me with tears. I feel my father's hands around my throat, every lie I've ever told spewing from his mouth.

I wear three pink carnations in my hair. My father prays the bottom flower will die first. He wants me to live a life attentive to the echoes of wood snapping in the forest.

VI

My pores open, a rotting stench filling the room. My body releases memories of you hidden in my ovaries, crouching behind a malignant cyst. I won't remember my ripe cherry softening tissues thrown in wastebaskets, your consideration between my legs overwhelming.

I shift my focus to the open window, the smell of the swamp wafting in my face. I hear your footsteps in the piles of leaves, your shoes coated with the blistered skin of a forgotten lover. You forced her to dance, wearing nothing but red-hot iron slippers, her body collapsing, thrown with the burning coals.

Later, you will creep into my bedroom and replace the photos of us with statues of the Virgin, her bare feet crushing the black serpent who threatened me to light candles for every dead soul refused a grave.

VII

Let them eat cake! my mother shouts as she walks to the guillotine. She steps on the executioner's shoe, apologizes for her ineptness, her hands tied behind her back with the sharp tongue of a dead queen.

Frosted-pink roses and frozen strawberries sowed from the tears of Venus decorate the cake.

A blushing discharge evades the hole between my legs, its curdled chunks resembling cottage cheese.

You howl beneath the yellow moon in the night sky, a warning to look out for predators, their mouths already gnawing on the necks of small animals.

Your expulsion does not mean I will forever forbid you from owning my innocence.

Tell Me About Yourself

My mouth is dry; the interviewer doesn't offer me a refreshment. I look down at my hands again. The late afternoon sky darkens, and I realize I won't hit heavy traffic on the way home.

Notes

In "Playing Along," the line, "...reminds me why she was naked from the waist down, her body lying on a rock wall in a field a hundred yards away from her abandoned shoe, her red coat shielding her perpetrator's remorse..." is influenced by the unsolved homicide of Katherine "Kathy" Kolodziej.

In "Maiden in the Tower," the line, "I can dream about my dead grandmother and believe I will solve the problem" is inspired by a dream interpretation found on www.dreamchrist.com.

In "Three Hail Marys," the line, "I can't be like her, an adolescent who watched Christ throw his head back and take her nipple and areola into his mouth" is inspired by Kaitlin Hardy Shetler's poem "Sometimes I Wonder." The line, "When your father dies, I won't turn my face to the wall," is inspired by Aurelia Plath recounting the moment Sylvia Plath learned about her father's passing.

The title, "Faithful Daughter," is named after an interpretation of my name found on behindthename.com through a discussion forum. The line, "Instead, I dream I am a nun living in the 1400s, biting the other sisters of the convent," is inspired by a report of a nun who started biting her companions in a German convent in the 1400s. The line, "Don't I deserve to wear a garland on my head, surrendered to the truth that was patient enough to wait for me?" is inspired by Edna St. Vincent Millay's "Sonnet 85." The line, "...until the danger turns into a door," is inspired by @persinette via Instagram.

The title, "Flannan Isles Lighthouse," is named after the Flannan Isles Lighthouse mystery.

The title, "Premonition for the Devouring Female," is taken from a dream interpretation found on www.dreamaboutmeaning.com.

"When Resentments Create Delusions" is after a poem by Amalia Kahn.

Acknowledgments

Thank you to Verses Magazine for publishing "A List Describing Home" and The Luna Collective for publishing "Secrets."

Thank you to my family and friends. Their continual support and love always reminds me how grateful I am for the life I have.

Thank you to my pups. I can always rely on our walks to help clear my head. And thank you to my cats for the endless biscuits, kisses, and headbutts.

Thank you to Michael. I don't even think saying thank you is enough for all he does for me.

Thank you to Patrick Zavorskas, my editor, for caring about my work as much as I do.

Thank you to Alise Versella, Frankie Balzano, and Jessica Ballen for their beautiful blurbs. I am so thankful to call these lovely writers my friends.

And thank you to Querencia Press and Emily Perkovich. After many rejections, I felt defeated, but Querencia proved that when one door closes, another one opens.